NORTHUMBRIA

NORTHUMBRIA

A COLLECTION AND A RECOLLECTION

Photographs by David Bell
Text by Brian Redhead

Constable · London

First published in Great Britain 1987
by Constable and Company Limited
10 Orange Street London WC2H 7EG
Copyright © 1987 text by Brian Redhead
Copyright © 1987 photographs by David Bell
Reprinted 1988, 1990
ISBN 0 09 467980 0
Printed and bound in Spain by
Graficas Estella, S.A.

A CIP catalogue record for this book
is available from the British Library

For

WILFRID BELL

CONTENTS

INTRODUCTION

WHEN I was seven, and supposed to be asleep, I would sit at the bedroom window in our house in Newcastle and look out across Northumberland to the Cheviot Hills and to what is now the Northumberland National Park. This, I knew, was the real North.

Now, fifty years later, I sit and write in the upper room of a farm cottage above Macclesfield in Cheshire and look out onto the Peak National Park whose boundary is the next lane. This, I tell visitors from the South, is the North.

Bede, sitting in his cell in Jarrow, would have agreed. For him the most important frontier in the land did not lie between the Tyne and the Solway where the Romans had put it, nor between the Tweed and the Solway where the Middle Ages were to leave it, but between the Humber and the Dee. That was the North-South divide. To the south of the Humber lay the kingdom of the southern English, sometimes called the Southumbrians. To the north of the Humber lay the kingdom of the Northumbrians, and Bede knew which he preferred. For him as for me, the North is that part of England which is dominated by the Pennines. The South is the rest.

The Pennines are the North. Northumbria is (or was) everything to the east of them and quite a lot to the west of them, Carlisle, for instance, and even Chester, on occasion. And for more than a century Northumbria was the centre of European civilization.

The Vikings put an end to that when they sacked the monastery of Lindisfarne in AD 793 and Northumbria has shrunk since then in almost every sense. It is now confined to the geographical counties of Northumberland and Durham, with perhaps a foothold in what we used to call the North Riding. Anyone writing to Bede at Jarrow would now have to add to the address the designation Tyne and Wear, and who would dare to assert that it is still the centre of European civilization?

To appreciate Northumbria now, all that is necessary is to revel in its landscape and to revere its past. It helps if you go there in person and this book is meant to encourage you to see it for yourself.

The landscape of Northumbria is there to be looked at. To enjoy it, it is not essential to know the difference between Silurian rock and Andesetic lava or that the Great Whin Sill which stretches from Bamburgh to Greenhead is an igneous intrusion. I once heard a girl at the youth hostel at Bellingham ask innocently about the ingenious rock.

Too many guide books to Northumbria confront the readers with a geological intrusion which causes them to read no further and they never get to know about Oswald and Aidan. But it does excite the mind to know that Cheviot is the stump of an ancient volcano. Miss Eggie told us that in the reception class at Pendower Elementary School, which is why I used to sit at the bedroom window on a summer's evening in the faint hope that Cheviot would erupt again.

Not that it needed to for it is an enchantment in itself. The Cheviot is 2,676 feet high (I know because Miss Eggie told me and we had no truck with metres in those days). I knew for myself that you could see it from Newcastle on a fine evening, and in earlier times it was an aid to navigation at sea. It beckoned princes of Denmark to the land of Bede, not always with desirable consequences.

Dales, moors, and scarplands lie between the uplands and the lowlands, and east of the Cheviots the scenery changes abruptly to the broad valleys of the Coquet and the Aln and the Breamish and the Till. Coquetdale running down to Rothbury is my favourite valley, though many people, I know, prefer Whittingham Vale above Alnwick.

Between the valleys and the lowland plain are the scarplands of the Kyloe Hills and Ros Castle, the Chillingham Ridge and Corby Crags, the Simonsides and Harbottle Crag. They face inwards towards the Cheviots and their summits provide the finest views in all Northumberland.

But Northumbria is both north and south of the Tyne, Northumberland and Durham, and the Tyne itself is two rivers, North and South, until they meet at Hexham. Some people think that the South Tyne valley is more spectacular than all the valleys of Northumberland. The river rises within two miles of the source of the Tees in Cumbria and crosses the county border close to Alston. It is travelling north-west at that point through some of the wildest land in England.

Walkers say that the Vales of Allen are the quintessential Northumbria, but they would because motorists cannot get near the best bits. The Allen rivers, which are not North and South but East and West, meet at Cupola Bridge and downstream from there, as I recall, is for the walker only. The motorist can drive to Plankey Mill where the narrow land ends and he has to turn back, but the main road crosses the river at Cupola Bridge and even a glimpse of the wild stream there is enough to

confirm that this is rare country. Indeed, the walk south from Plankey Mill is rough and dangerous when the river is high.

But every valley in Northumbria is its own reward – Weardale upstream of Bishop Auckland, Teesdale upstream of Barnard Castle, the Derwent Valley almost all the way from Blanchland to Blaydon. These are the valleys of Northumbria that are least known to those outside. Perhaps the time has come to designate a new National Park in the North Pennines.

If it is not stretching a point, there is even a serious case for arguing that a new North Pennine National Park should stretch from the northern boundary of the Yorkshire Dales National Park to the southern boundary of the Northumberland National Park to create a great Northern Territory to be conserved, enhanced, and enjoyed – not ours, as the slogan says, but ours to look after.

For the moment, the Northumberland National Park is only 398 choice square miles of Northumbria, seventy per cent of it open moorland, twenty per cent coniferous forest. And that is quite enough forest. Together with those immediately outside the Park, Northumberland's forests are among the largest in Europe.

The most recently published guide to the Park rightly says that because it is the least populated and the least visited of the ten National Parks in England and Wales, it is ideal for people seeking solitude in a remote landscape. It is, provided that they do not wander into the Otterburn Training Area. This, the largest military training area in the north of England, occupies no less than twenty-two per cent of the area of the National Park. The live firing ranges are used on anything from 250 to 300 days every year, when they are closed to public access. The military even wanted to plough a mock target airstrip for bombing training, but the Park

Authority would have none of it.

They were no less firm when it was proposed that high level nuclear waste should be buried in the Park in the Threestoneburn and Uswayford forests. Scarcely anyone goes there, was the argument. Scarcely anyone would if the Atomic Energy Authority had its way, was the reply. Anyway, as I said at the time, if the stuff is so safe why don't they bury it in the cellar at Number Ten?

However, in spite of the fir trees and the fusiliers, the Park remains a landscape of wide, open spaces where access is unrivalled and solitude easily found. It has the lowest density of population in England and Wales. Forestry and firing ranges apart, its remoteness has saved it from development, and conservation is essential to maintain both the landscape and the wildlife. You can see wild goats and night otters, wild geese and even the goosander. And the wild flowers range from the monkey flower to the Grass of Parnassus.

But the National Park ought to stretch to the sea. The Northumberland coast from north of the Coquet to south of the Tweed has been designated a Coastal Area of Outstanding Natural Beauty. And it is. It is a coastline every inch as beautiful as the Pembrokeshire coast, which, very properly, is a National Park. And a walk along the full length of the Northumberland coast, like a walk along the Pembrokeshire coast, is a conquest in itself.

South of the Coquet, from Amble down to the Long Sands at Tynemouth and beyond the Tyne to Roker and Crimdon and Redcar on Sea, the Northumbria coast, though not as beautiful as the northernmost stretch, is a string of holiday resorts. Some, like Tynemouth and Whitley Bay, have attracted visitors since people first took holidays. Others have taken it up of necessity.

I remember going to Newbiggin-by-the-Sea thirty odd years ago to write an article for the *Newcastle Evening Chronicle*. The guide book, I wrote, is blunt but out of date. Newbiggin, it says, is a mining and fishing village, but the colliery is soon to close, and the inshore fishing is almost at a standstill. Can it find new life as a holiday resort?

At the time it looked far from encouraging. Newbiggin Bay is a great semi-circle facing south so that its headlands lie east to west. The east promontory on which the Church of St Bartholomew stands was once a natural breakwater, but as the colliery working spread underground the headland rocks were undermined and gradually submerged. The unchecked waves rolling into the bay had washed the sand into the western end leaving the fishermen's beach, once soft and clean, ugly and spread with stones. Subsidence was also causing the crescent of houses above the foreshore to crack, and even though the local colliery was to close the coal was still to be worked from a nearby colliery. Until the subsidence was checked no one dare develop anything.

And if I remember rightly there was also a plan to build a new colliery railway on the edge of the town. It was to run through a cornfield which separated the last row of cottages in Newbiggin from the lovely church of Woodhorn. The cottages were called Church View. The locals were threatening to change the name to Railway View.

The article I wrote was headlined 'Doomed', but I was wrong. Today the guide book can describe Newbiggin as a developing resort where the young people of the county learn to sail, and the old still gather sea coal.

As a young reporter I lived in Tynemouth, lodging in Hotspur Street with Eva Fry, whose father, Old Mr Fry, danced the Lancers on his ninetieth birthday and rode a tandem bicycle with Eva until he was ninety-three. He built boats in the winter and took trippers round St Mary's lighthouse in the summer for seventy years. He walked the length of the beach every day and if there was no one in earshot he would sing the songs of Old Tynemouth, songs like this:

And now as I wander the old beach alone,
The waves seem to whisper the names that are gone,
'Twas there with my Alice I walked hand in hand,
While the wild waves in moonlight leant o'er the bright sand.
And sweet were the echoes of the dark cliffs above,
But oh sweeter her voice as she murmured her love.

The old man knew dozens of sentimental ditties like that, all about Tynemouth. There was one which went:

Other lands may be fairer but naught can be seen,
Like the shore where our first love and boyhood have been.
Oh give me the cliffs and the wild roaring sea,
The cliffs of Old Tynemouth forever for me.

There was another which began:

Where the sable seaweed's growing
Tynemouth on thy rocky shore,
'Tis sweet to hear the wild wind blowing
And the restless ocean roar . . .

And it ended:

. . . Where yon Abbey ruin stands hoary
And the dead in silence sleep.

I liked that one and would recite it when I took a nightly walk to the ruined Priory which is the pride of Tynemouth.

Eva's favourite, which she had in pokerwork above the mantelpiece read:

Cullercoats for fisher folk,
North Shields for its rags,
Tynemouth for canny folk,
And Preston for its nags.

Eva was cat mad, worse than me. She once spotted two small boys swinging a cat on the edge of the cliff, on the point of throwing it onto the rocks below. She leapt out of her car, picked up both boys by the heads as if they were ten-pin bowls, and had to be prevented (by me) from casting both of them to their deaths. But she was masterly at thinking up excuses if I was out of touch with the News Desk at the *Chronicle*.

It was at this time, between National Service and University, that I first began to think out loud about Northumbria. It is one thing to enjoy a place, quite another to explain why.

At school, the Royal Grammar School, the choice had always been between the Coast and the Wall. On a day trip we cycled to the Coast and wandered round Cullercoats and Whitley Bay. But at half-term we cycled to the Wall and lodged in the youth hostels at Acomb and Once Brewed. We also went to Bellingham because that was the only hostel where the warden did not live in and you could get up to mischief at night.

Hadrian's Wall is the greatest monument to the Romans in Britain, and one of the finest historical monuments in the world. I have introduced countless people to it, and not one of them has been disappointed. We used to park our bikes at Once Brewed and then walk the Wall, telling each other bad jokes in bad Latin, invariably ending with someone saying Pollux.

A friend made a film about the Wall while we were still at school. It won an award and determined his subsequent career. From that day to this it has never entered my head to drive from Carlisle to Newcastle, or vice versa, by any route other than the Military Road.

(Though, in truth, there are only two to choose between.) The Military Road was not built by the Romans, but by General Wade in the 1750s so that he might take on the Jacobites, and he stole bits of the Wall for his purpose. It provides the best view of the Wall, other than on foot, and the best introduction to Northumbria for someone in a hurry. It is like riding across the top of the world and sharing it only with the ancient gods. And you can always stop at Chollerford for tea, where a waitress once asked a customer if she would like the gateau cake.

The senior history master at the RGS in my time was Mr S. Middlebrook, known to all Old Novos as Sammy even though his first name was Sidney. Sammy wrote the most authoritative history of Newcastle yet published, but at school, because of the pressures of the syllabus, he had to teach us about the Thirty Years War and the territorial ambitions of Charles V. He taught me about Newcastle in one day on a walk through the city.

It was in the long vacation in 1953. The editor of the *Chronicle* had kindly taken me on for the holiday to supplement my student grant, and I had persuaded him to let me write a series of articles to be called 'The Heritage of Newcastle'. Heritage was not then an over-used word, though this may have been the beginning of its downfall. Armed with enough expenses to buy him lunch, I invited Mr Middlebrook to show me round the city. It was a day I was never to forget.

I had already written the introduction to the series, a rather lofty piece ticking off the city council for not caring as much about the heritage as I did. I dismissed the official city guide book as being little more than circumspect. I even chided the citizens for their indifference. Then I went on my walk with Mr Middlebrook.

I was to learn that day that the city in which I had been born and brought up was far more interesting than even I had imagined. We walked the city walls which once encircled Newcastle. They were built during the Scottish Wars and when complete were over two miles long with seven main gates, nineteen towers, and countless turrets.

We came upon a fine section of the walls at the back of a brewer's yard in Orchard Street which had just been cleaned by a mason called Joe Smart, who had been hired by the Corporation for the task, and whose knowledge of medieval Newcastle was scholarly. We saw the four towers and the two turrets on the west walls between Westgate Road and Gallowgate. Durham Tower was tucked out of sight then, but the other three, the Heber Tower, the Morden Tower and even the Ever Tower, stood in an imposing line behind Stowell Street, and I had never seen them before. We saw the Plummer Tower and the Corner Tower and the Sallyport Gate and suddenly I had a grasp of this walled city which was once the most densely populated city in England outside London.

Then we moved inside the walls, first to Blackfriars where work had just begun, inspired by the Society for the Protection of Ancient Buildings, to restore what remained of the monastery. I knew the place. I had clattered across the cloisters where the Black Friars had once walked on my way to the Match on many a Saturday afternoon to watch Jackie Milburn and Len Shackleton. What I did not know until then was that in spite of years of misuse and neglect the remains were as extensive as those of any Dominican house in England.

Then we went to the Keelmen's Hospital, the only almshouse in Britain built by the poor for themselves. The keelmen who carried the coal in keels from the quays to the colliers berthed downstream raised the money themselves in 1701 by levying a penny on every keel-load carried. As children we had all sung 'The Keel Row'.

But this was the first time I had even been in the Hospital. Very few people had in those days. The last keelman, Old Geordie Tulip, who had been caretaker of the Hospital, had died only three years earlier in 1950. The rooms in the Hospital, which is built round a courtyard like a medieval college, were let out as tenements at a rent then of half a crown a week, and the City Corporation which owned it had no plans for it. It was dismissed in one sentence in the official city guide book and when I mentioned back at the *Chronicle* office that I had been there, one old reporter said I must be joking because everyone knew that the Keelmen's Hospital had fallen down years ago. No wonder I became a passionate conservationist.

However, everyone in Newcastle even then knew about the Keep of the Castle. You couldn't miss it. It was, and is, the most famous building in the city and a well-preserved historical monument, largely due to the efforts of the Newcastle Society of Antiquaries who had leased it a hundred years previously and had restored and taken good care of it. They had also leased the Black Gate which housed the Society's library and collection.

But when Mr Middlebrook and I walked from one to the other on that day we found that their surroundings, which were the responsibility of the Corporation, were a disgrace. The site was not just neglected and overgrown but there were great ugly unwanted concrete air-raid shelters down the Side, and the Heron Pit was housed in a black wooden lean-to that looked like a coal shed.

Castle Garth was a dirty drab square and the Castle and the Keep looked as if they had grown on refuse tips. All this I recorded faithfully in the *Chronicle* and every time I go back to Newcastle now I salute the improvements.

Even more depressing then was what we discovered on the quayside. This was the heart of the medieval borough and the centre of the city's government then was the Guildhall. It was still there and somebody had just got round to putting up the sign saying Guildhall. But there was no further information and the other plates alongside indicating the presence within of a commercial exchange and a probation office did nothing to attract visitors.

It was even worse at No. 41 Sandgate. This is the best known address in Newcastle. It was the home of Bessie Surtees, who in 1772 escaped from the upper casement and down a ladder into the arms of her lover John Scott. Why she bothered I have never understood because he became Lord Eldon and one of the most reactionary Lord Chancellors in our history. But love is blind.

Mr Middlebrook and I found it as difficult to get into No. 41 as Bessie Surtees had to get out. The house then was divided between flats on the upper floors and offices on the lower floors. It was understandable that neither the flat dwellers nor the office workers would want to be disturbed, but the first floor, from which Bessie had descended, was actually empty at the time and yet no one then thought it appropriate to make arrangements to admit the public.

I denounced this too in the subsequent article and then went on to point out that Newcastle was (and is) one of the few cities which can lay claim to a birthplace. It is Bridge End, the city side of the Swing Bridge. There the Romans built their bridge and the Normans after them.

In all, five successive bridges have spanned the river at that point. It was there that Newcastle was born. Someone, I wrote, should erect a plaque on the spot saying just that.

Someone in the Town Hall wrote a dismissive letter to my editor in reply. Who, it asked, could possibly be interested? We have come a long way since then, and no one visiting Newcastle now can fail to discover as much as they seek to know about that marvellous city. Nor can they know Northumbria without getting to know Newcastle.

But not everyone thirty years ago was dismissive of the past. The previous summer I had gone to write a piece about Wallington Hall. It was then the home of Sir Charles Trevelyan, at eighty-two the last surviving member of the first Labour Government. He greeted me in the uniform of radical English socialists, tweed knickerbockers and brown boots. He showed me round and I only wish that tape recorders had existed then for a recording of what he said would delight every visitor to the Hall today.

Wallington is the finest house in the Wansbeck Valley. There was a border castle there in the Middle Ages and later a Tudor house probably similar to Belsay or Chipchase. In those days it belonged to the Fenwicks, as most things in Northumberland did, but when Sir John Fenwick was executed for conspiring against William III, it was sold to Sir William Blackett, a Newcastle merchant. Blackett was no conservationist. He pulled down the old castle and the Tudor house and built the new Wallington.

Fortunately he chose a moment when English domestic architecture was about to flower and Wallington is a simple, elegant and imposing mansion. I remember that Sir Charles told me that the surroundings must have been hideous for the land had been laid waste by the border warfare of the previous centuries. But after Sir William Blackett died, his successor Sir Walter Blackett, a Calverley who changed his name, laid out the land around to give the Hall a setting worthy of its design. He also brought in Italian plasterers to decorate the house and their work is

unblemished to this day.

He died childless and the Hall passed to his sister Julia, who married a Trevelyan. There has only been one great change in the house since, other than giving it to the National Trust. In the middle of the last century Pauline, Lady Trevelyan, made Wallington a centre of artistic society. Swinburne read his poems there, Millais painted his pictures, Ruskin, who was good at neither, talked – and suggested that the inner courtyard, which was dark and dingy, should be covered in. The present beautifully lit picture gallery and central hall are his inspiration, and Bell Scott, the Pre-Raphaelite painter who was then teaching in Newcastle, painted eight pictures telling the story of Northumbria from the building of Hadrian's Wall to the erection of Stephenson's High Level Bridge.

After Wallington there was no stopping me and I rushed off to Raby which I had only seen from the road. Once the south-west Durham home of the lordly Nevilles, it remains a perfect and unrivalled example of a feudal stronghold. Set in an extensive park, in which red deer roam and hunters exercise, it is a many towered castle, solid and enduring, with no two towers alike, and no external ornament to distort its grandeur.

The Nevilles had so many castles that they could live in a different one every week of the year. They were a turbulent family who ruled the North, fought the Percys, sired kings, and thought themselves more powerful than the Crown.

In the Baron's Hall at Raby on 13 November 1567 the last of the Nevilles summoned a Great Council of northern noblemen. They pledged their support for Mary Queen of Scots and the Church of Rome against Elizabeth I and the Church of England. But the Rising of the North was crushed and Raby, like all the Neville estates, became the property of the Crown. Elizabeth sent her royal commissioners to inspect the castle. It is, they said, a monstrous old abbey which will soon decay, which shows how much they knew.

James I sold Raby Castle, and Barnard Castle, to Sir Henry Vane, whose son, also Henry, got over-excited in the Civil War, trailed his conscience, and was eventually executed by Charles II who found him too much. Pepys said he was a martyr and a saint. His son Christopher was more pragmatic, and he started the family's collection of titles: Barons Barnard, Earls of Darlington, Dukes of Cleveland. But the fourth Duke died without an heir and all the titles except the Barony of Barnard became extinct.

When I visited Raby it was the home of the tenth Baron, albeit a ninety-two roomed home, and I vowed that if I ever became a baron and an earl and a duke I too would have a home like that. As a student I could look no higher than Lumley.

Lumley Castle is falling down, said the headlines of my schooldays, and had the castle not found a new use it might very well have fallen into ruin. From the Chester-le-Street bypass across the river to the east, it always looked good, but it would have decayed if University College, Durham, had not decided to seal its reputation as the only university college in the world with two genuine medieval castles as its halls of residence, Durham and Lumley.

The Norman castle of the Prince Bishops of Durham stands in Durham City itself not far from the great cathedral and is best first glimpsed from the train. The Bishops of Durham now live all year round in Auckland Castle at Bishop Auckland, which in Norman times and for many centuries thereafter was their country retreat. The private chapel there was built in 1665 from the ruins of the twelfth century Banqueting Hall.

Lumley is more self-effacing than Durham. The Lumleys liked a peaceful life so they minded their own business, fought no one, and their castle is one of the few that has never been beseiged. But it is haunted.

Lily of Lumley, the wife of the fifteenth-century Lord, was thought to be a heretic, and when her husband was away in the wars the monks of Finchale Abbey came to the castle to persuade her to recant. She refused and they tortured her to death. The discovery early this century of a skeleton in the castle revived the legend and when Lumley was first opened as a college hall of residence after the Second World War no local girls would come as maids. Eventually two were persuaded to start and, when they were neither bricked up in a cupboard nor thrown down a well, others soon followed. When I visited Lumley only a year or two after it had opened as a college hall, all the maids talked with daring familiarity about poor Lily.

My learning curve through the castles of Northumbria went back in time. To Alnwick, where the Percy family, the Dukes of Northumberland, have lived for nine centuries. To Warkworth, the finest ruin in Northumberland, where it is impossible not to think of Harry Hotspur and to recite the words that Shakespeare wrote for him. (When Michael Redgrave played Hotspur at Stratford he came to Northumberland to learn to speak the words as a Percy would. Half the audience at Stratford that year could not understand a word he said.) To Dunstanburgh where it is best to leave the car at Embleton and walk south-east to the castle, a ruin now, but the largest castle in Northumerland.

Finally I went to Bamburgh, royal Bamburgh. From every approach this king of Northumbrian castles, rugged as the ancient kingdom over which it once held sway, stands out as the most majestic and impregnable of strongholds. This is the capital of Northumbria and the cradle of Northumbrian history.

There is only one drawback over the

drawbridge; the castle is a reproduction, rebuilt by the first Lord Armstrong from its original foundations, not restored but reconstructed. If history has been unkind to Bamburgh, Bamburgh is now unkind to history. But neither time nor history can take away its perfect setting.

It was Flaming Ida, the Saxon monarch and founder of the Northumbrian kings, who first built a castle there and from the sixth to the sixteenth century Bamburgh was beset by feuds and war. When William the Conquerer harried the North, Bamburgh was the only inhabited town left standing in Northumberland. When the North rebelled, Robert Mowbray, Earl of Northumberland, held the castle against William Rufus. Mowbray was tricked into leaving Bamburgh and was taken prisoner, but his wife Matilda held out until the King threatened to gouge out her husband's eyes before the castle wall. She surrendered.

Scottish and English kings occupied the castle in turn. In the Wars of the Roses it was a Lancastrian stronghold and Henry VI lived in it for nine miserable months, constantly beseiged by the Earl of Warwick. But when the Tudors finally captured the English throne and settled the kingdom, Bamburgh was left in peace. In fact no one knew what to do with it.

Lord Crewe, the last of the Prince Bishops of Durham, bought it in 1704 and redeemed an inconsequential life by founding the Bamburgh Charities. They built a charity school within the castle walls for thirty-four little girls, one of whom was Grace Darling, the heroic daughter of the lighthouse keeper on the Farne Islands. That school was pulled down when Armstrong rebuilt the castle. The twelve-hundred-year-old draw-well, hewn through 150 feet of solid rock, is the only continuous link with Bamburgh's beginnings.

Oswald supped from the well and Aidan too. Oswald, a convert to Christianity, spent some early years in exile on Iona, and when he regained the Northumbrian throne he sent to Iona for monks to spread the Gospel. Columba came first to Lindisfarne and established a monastery there. There were no stone buildings then, just thatched huts to sleep in, and small chapels for prayer. The monks now led by Aidan walked the lanes of Northumbria talking to everyone they met and converting as many as they could. Aidan reported regularly to Oswald and often had supper with him in the castle.

Cuthbert followed Aidan and was the great conciliator in the dispute between the Celtic rites and the Roman rites which was settled in favour of Rome at the Synod of Whitby. Cuthbert reconciled the monks at Lindisfarne to the change. He was thought to have the gift of healing and large numbers of people streamed across the sands at low tide to receive his blessing. None, says Bede, had to carry back home the burdens with which he arrived.

Cuthbert gradually withdrew from the community and became a hermit, first on a tiny island off Lindisfarne, now called St Cuthbert's Island, and then on the Inner Farne. But the people still came and he was forced to build a landing stage and a little guest house. He was dragged from there to be a bishop at the request of King Egfrith and at the insistence of the Church.

For two years Cuthbert travelled the kingdom that was becoming the envy of Europe, the kingdom of Alcuin, the teacher of Charlemagne, of Caedmon, the visionary cowherd-poet, of Bede, the first and greatest of historians. Its monasteries were to produce the best illuminated manuscripts in Europe, the best standing stone crosses, the best garnet and gold metalwork, the best poetry – but, above all, the saintliest of men. This was a civilization with a soul.

And in AD 687 when Cuthbert felt death

coming on he withdrew again to the Inner Farne to contemplate the inner life. There they found him dying and they brought his body back to Lindisfarne for burial. Eleven years later when his body was elevated to a new shrine it was found to be incorruptible. And when the Danes destroyed Lindisfarne the monks fled with the shrine and the relics. They carried them through the years to Norham, to Ripon, to Chester-le-Street, and finally to Durham in AD 995 where they have rested ever since, first in a Saxon church and then from 1083 in the new Norman cathedral.

Durham Cathedral was recently voted the best building in the world, and I would not quarrel with that. One Sunday evening last Advent, I travelled with the Bishop of Durham from his home at Auckland Castle to the Cathedral for the Processional Service. And sitting in the darkness of that great church, where services have been sung every day for so many centuries, with the choir moving by candlelight from station to station, I found it took no great effort of the imagination to believe that Northumbria is still the centre of European civilization.

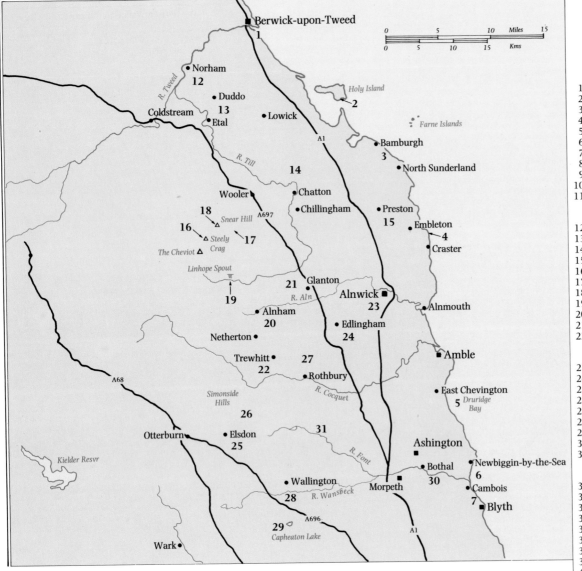

Northumbria

The Coast

1 Berwick-upon-Tweed: the Elizabethan Walls
2 Lindisfarne Castle, Holy Island
3 Bamburgh Castle
4 Dunstanburgh Castle
5 East Chevington
6 Newbiggin-by-the-Sea
7 Cambois Power Station from north Blyth
8 Cullercoats Bay
9 Lighthouse, Lizard Point, near Whitburn
10 Roker sea front
11 Middlesbrough, the transporter bridge

North Northumberland and the Cheviots

12 Norham Castle
13 Duddo Stones
14 Chatton Park hill
15 Preston Tower
16 Steely Crag
17 Harthope valley
18 Sheep pens on Snear Hill
19 View from Linhope Spout, Cheviots
20 Alnham Church and vicar's pele
21 The Cheviots from the Glanton-Powburn road
22 Netherton and the Cheviots from Trewhitt

From the Aln to the Wansbeck

23 Alnwick Castle
24 Edlingham Castle
25 Elsdon: the vicars pele
26 Simonside Hills from the road to Elsdon
27 The moors above Rothbury
28 Wallington Hall
29 Capheaton Lake
30 Bothal Castle
31 The River Font

The Tyne Valley and Hadrian's Wall

32 The Tyne Bridges
33 Amstrong Bridge and Holy Trinity Church
34 Bywell: Saxon Tower of St. Andrew's Church
35 Bywell Castle
36 The vicar's pele at Corbridge
37 Hexham Abbey
38 Near Wallhouses
39 Standing Stone Farm near Matfen
40 Roman wall west of Milecastle 29
41 Peel Crags on the Roman Wall
42 Turret near Sewingshields
43 Crag Lough
44 Roman Wall at Walltown Crags
45 The Irthing Valley from Birdoswald
46 Chipchase Castle
47 Langley Castle

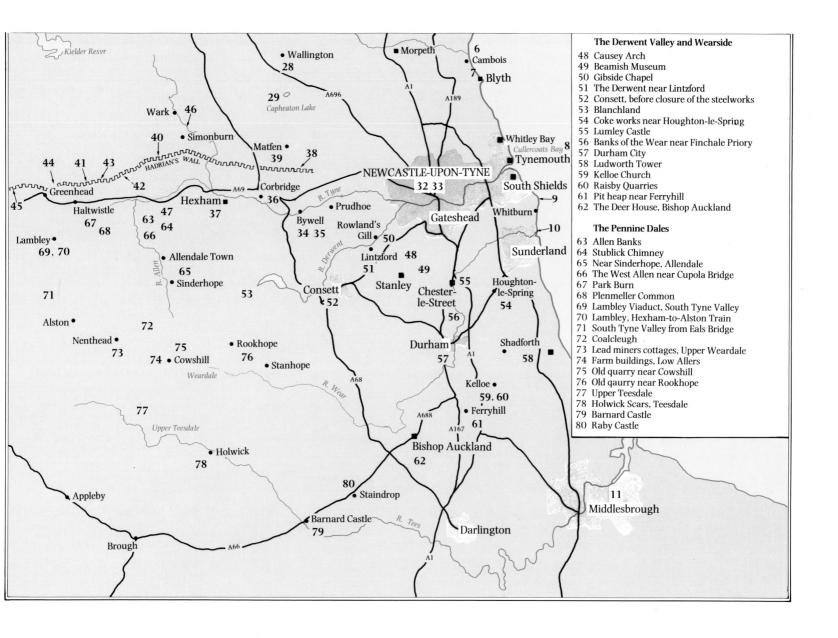

The Derwent Valley and Wearside
48 Causey Arch
49 Beamish Museum
50 Gibside Chapel
51 The Derwent near Lintzford
52 Consett, before closure of the steelworks
53 Blanchland
54 Coke works near Houghton-le-Spring
55 Lumley Castle
56 Banks of the Wear near Finchale Priory
57 Durham City
58 Ludworth Tower
59 Kelloe Church
60 Raisby Quarries
61 Pit heap near Ferryhill
62 The Deer House, Bishop Auckland

The Pennine Dales
63 Allen Banks
64 Stublick Chimney
65 Near Sinderhope, Allendale
66 The West Allen near Cupola Bridge
67 Park Burn
68 Plenmeller Common
69 Lambley Viaduct, South Tyne Valley
70 Lambley, Hexham-to-Alston Train
71 South Tyne Valley from Eals Bridge
72 Coalcleugh
73 Lead miners cottages, Upper Weardale
74 Farm buildings, Low Allers
75 Old quarry near Cowshill
76 Old qaurry near Rookhope
77 Upper Teesdale
78 Holwick Scars, Teesdale
79 Barnard Castle
80 Raby Castle

The Coast

To be brought up with a bucket and spade on a beach
in Northumbria, as anyone who built his first sandcastle
at Tynemouth or Seaton Sluice, at Beadnell or
Bamburgh, will affirm, is to be privileged. The coast of
Northumbria is not only the best introduction to the
North-East of England, it is among the best introductions
to life. Down the full length of the coast, from the Tweed
to the Tees, the sand is smooth, the dunes are seductive,
the cliffs dramatic, the castles historic. This is what a
coastline should be, a place of beauty at which men and
women and children have marvelled for centuries. New
every morning is the love that people have for these
shores, and Cuthbert would still recognize the place.

Berwick-upon-Tweed (1)

Part of the city walls built in the Italian style
in the reign of Elizabeth I.

Lindisfarne Castle (2)

The building owes its present shape to the
work carried out in 1903 by Sir Edwin
Lutyens.

Bamburgh Castle (3)

It is perched on an abrupt outcrop of the Whin
Sill with long clean beaches and dunes
stretching away to north and south. Better
outside than in.

Dunstanburgh Castle (4)

Since 1380 when John of Gaunt turned the
gate into a keep this, the largest castle in
Northumberland, has been neither altered nor
improved.

East Chevington (5)

This yellow-brick colliery village near Druridge
Bay has now been replaced by an open-cast
coal site. A quarter of a mile from here is the
vast sweep of Druridge Bay, a five-mile stretch
of beach and sand dunes on which it is
proposed to build a nuclear power station.

Newbiggin-by-the-Sea (6)

Gathering sea-coal is a traditional form of
family income supplement.

Cambois (pronounced Camuss) (7)

The power station seen from the ferry landing at North Blyth.

Cullercoats Bay (8)

The American artist Winslow Homer lived
here in the 1880s, painting scenes of the local
fishing community. This was the view from his
studio at No. 12 Bank Top.

Lighthouse, Lizard Point (9)

Between South Shields and Whitburn.

Roker, Sunderland (10)

Play area on the sea front.

Middlesbrough (11)

The transporter bridge has been described as the town's most impressive building. Built in 1911 it is the largest of its kind in the world.

North Northumbria
and the Cheviots

Cheviot is a Celtic word, because the Celts took to the
hills of Northumbria when the Angles invaded and left
the lush valleys to the newcomers. Ask anyone now, not
from these parts, to name a Cheviot hill other than The
Cheviot itself and they will usually pass. Not for them a
passing knowledge of Braydon Crag and Hedgehope,
Cushat Law and Comb Fell, Windy Gyle and Bloody Bush
Edge – all of them over two thousand feet. This is a
territory which can be admired from afar but only
explored on foot. And even the Celts were newcomers
here in their time. Earlier inhabitants walked these hills
and left their circles and their burial mounds to prove it.
Centuries later the people preferred the riverbanks and
they fought for possession at Flodden Field.

Norham Castle (12)

Norham, on the south bank of the Tweed, was
a northern outpost of the county Palatine of
Durham whose Bishop, Hugh Pudsey,
commissioned the castle in 1158.

Duddo (13)

A mile to the north of the village lies a small
pre-historic stone circle. All but the most
curious will be deterred from reaching the site,
if not by the ghoulish scarecrow then by the
lack of any path through the cultivated field
which surrounds it.

Chatton Park Hill (14)

$2\frac{1}{2}$ miles north of Chillingham Park, home of
the famous herd of wild white cattle.

Preston Tower (15)

Near Ellingham. Originally this was a square
tower with four corner turrets like a small
version of Langley Castle. The clock was added
in the last century, giving the building the look
of a piece of Staffordshire pottery. Privately
owned but open to the public.

Steely Crag (16)

An outcrop in the northern Cheviots.

Harthope Valley (17)

Looking south-east to Happy Valley from
Snear Hill.

Sheep Pens (18)

Near Carey Burn in the Cheviots.

Linhope Burn (19)

A view from the head of Linhope Spout in the eastern Cheviots.

Alnham Church and Pele Tower (20)

This small village lies in a hollow on the south-western edge of the Cheviots. Both St Michael's Church and the Vicar's Pele were restored in the last century.

The Cheviots (21)

View from the road between Powburn and
Glanton.

View from Trewhitt (22)

With Netherton Burn Foot in the middle
distance and the Cheviots on the horizon.

From the Aln to the Wansbeck

Northumbria runs with rivers and the three which spill
into the sea in mid-Northumberland, the Aln and the
Coquet and the Wansbeck, inscribe valleys of
unsurpassed beauty. These are valleys where people love
to live. They call them dales and they have occupied
them for centuries. Alnwick (pronounced Ann'ick), the
town on the clear water, commands the Aln and
commands Northumberland, though where there were
once fifty inns there are now only half that number.
Rothbury, high up Coquetdale, is one of oldest
settlements in Northumberland, and was a sizeable place
in Cuthbert's time. And the people of Morpeth on the
Wansbeck thought so highly of their town that in 1215
they burned it down rather than let King John set foot
in it. Visitors now are welcome.

Alnwick Castle (23)

Ancestral home of Northumberland's most important family, the Percys, and occupied by the present Duke of Northumberland.

Edlingham Castle (24)

A tower-house with several features which make it more grand than most.

Elsdon (25)

The Vicar's Pele Tower from the churchyard.
On the edge of the village lies what Pevsner
described as 'the best Motte-and-Bailey castle
in Northumberland'.

The Simonside Hills (26)

Looking east from the Rothbury to Elsdon
road, near Billsmoor Park.

Near Rothbury (27)

From the town centre there is a pleasant five-mile walk which leads up onto the heather moors to the north. From here there are fine views of open country and the Cheviots.

Wallington Hall (28)

The finest house in the Wansbeck Valley. Built
in 1688 by Sir William Blackett. The
Trevelyan family made several alterations and
improvements, notably those of 1855
suggested by John Ruskin. A National Trust
property.

Capheaton, the Lake (29)

The grounds of Capheaton Hall were laid out
by Capability Brown who was born nearby at
Kirkharle. It was one of his earliest
commissions.

Bothal Castle (30)

A castle has stood on this site since Saxon
times but the present building is largely
fourteenth century. Not open to the public.

The River Font (31)

Also called the Font Burn.

The Tyne Valley
and Hadrian's Wall

Tyneside embraces the River Tyne from Scotswood to the sea, the industrial Tyne. Tynedale, or the Tyne Valley, is upstream from Wylam to Hexham, where within three miles the river divides into the North Tyne and the South Tyne each with a valley, and a beauty, and history of its own. But the Tyne Valley itself is both beautiful and historic. Prudoe has what is probably the oldest Keep in Northumbria. Bywell is one of the few villages anywhere with two churches, built by squabbling sisters. Corbridge sits astride the oldest road in Britain. And Hexham has had a cathedral since AD 681 when it was only the fifth stone church in Christendom north of the Alps. But the stone wall of Hadrian was already there. It is the greatest monument in the western world to the military power of Rome, and the longest tourist attraction in Britain.

The Tyne Bridges (32)

The great arch of the 'New Tyne Bridge' which was completed in 1928 has become the symbol of Tyneside. Robert Stephenson's double-deck 'High Level Bridge' of 1859 carries both road and rail traffic.

Armstrong Bridge (33)

And Holy Trinity Church, Jesmond, Newcastle.

Bywell (34)

The Saxon tower of Bywell St Andrew in this
village with two churches.

Bywell (35)

The castle, actually a fortified tower-house,
viewed from the gate of Bywell St Peter. Not
open to the public.

Corbridge (36)

The Vicar's Pele Tower of St Andrew's Church.

Hexham Abbey (37)

The Priory Church of St Wilfrid is largely early English with a Victorian eastern front. The Saxon crypt dates back to AD 674, when the first church on this site was begun.

Near Wallhouses (38)

Between the B6318 and Matfen.

Near Matfen (39)

Standing Stone Farm takes its name from the
seven-foot pre-historic Menhir known as
'Stub's Stone'.

The Roman Wall (40)

West of Milecastle 29.

_____

Peel Crags (41)

With Highshields Crags, Crag Lough, and in
the distance Hotbank Farm and Hotbank
Crags.

The Roman Wall (42)

Turret 34a near Sewingshields.

Crag Lough (43)

From Highshields Crags.

The Roman Wall (44)

At Walltown Crags. The north-facing
escarpment is part of a ridge of hard volcanic
rock known as the Great Whin Sill. The Farne
Islands and the cliffs of Bamburgh and
Dunstanburgh are outcrops of the same
intrusion.

The Irthing Valley (45)

From Birdoswald Fort on the Roman Wall.

Chipchase Castle (46)

The original fourteenth-century Pele Tower has gained several extensions including the splendid Jacobean east front. Not open to the public.

Langley Castle (47)

Langley is a superior example of the fortified tower-house. A print of 1884 shows it in semi-ruinous condition but it was sensibly restored round the turn of the century by Cadwallader Bates and today is a comfortable hotel.

The Derwent Valley and Wearside

To the outsider the name Derwent suggests the Lake
District not Northumbria, but to those in the know the
Derwent Valley is one of the most wooded valleys east of
the Pennines. The river rises near Blanchland, the
immaculate village of the white-robed monks, and joins
the River Tyne at Derwent Haugh near Blaydon. Its final
miles are plunged into industry or industrial dereliction
but its many miles upstream of Rowland's Gill are the
local motorists' delight. The Wear, like the Tyne, goes
down to the sea. Wearside, like Tyneside, is the industrial
end. Weardale is upstream of Bishop Auckland, wild
country in winter, green and welcoming in summer. But
between Weardale and Wearside is that part of the river
which curls round the city of Durham and is almost a
principality of its own.

Causey Arch (48)

This 105-foot span bridge was built in 1727 by a local stonemason, Ralph Wood. It carried the rails for horse-drawn coal wagons and is said to be the world's first railway bridge.

Beamish Museum (49)

Railway carriages awaiting restoration.

Gibside Chapel (50)

Built in the 1760s to the design of James Paine. A National Trust property.

The River Derwent (51)

Near Lintzford, west of Rowlands Gill.

Consett (52)

As it was during its dirty but prosperous
heyday.

Blanchland (53)

The village take its name from the twelfth-century abbey of 'white' monks. The irregular square of greystone houses was built by the Crewe estate about 1750.

Coke Works (54)

Near Houghton-le-Spring.

Lumley Castle (55)

A bold four-square picture-book castle, the
bulk of which dates from the fourteenth
century.

Woodland Walk (56)

On the bank of the River Wear near Finchale
Priory.

Durham (57)

A prospect of the city from a mile to the east,
by Old Durham farm.

Ludworth Tower (58)

Near Shadforth.

Church Kelloe (59)

The tower is Norman. Elizabeth Barrett
Browning was born nearby at Coxhoe Hall
and was baptized in this church in February
1808.

Raisby Quarries (60)

Between Coxhoe and Kelloe. Sometimes called 'Garmdondsway' Quarry after the medieval village of that name.

Pit Heap, near Ferryhill (61)

This attractive slag landscape is no more. A few years ago it was cleared and the land returned to agricultural use.

Deer House, Bishop Auckland (62)

This enclosure in the Gothick style was built
in 1767 as part of the landscaping of Auckland
Park, which adjoins the private residence of
the Bishop of Durham. The park itself is open
to the public without charge.

The Pennine Dales

The Tyne and the Tees empty into the sea thirty miles
apart, but they begin life within two miles of each other
high in the Pennines. The South Tyne runs north-east,
the Tees south-west, and the valleys of both are
spectacular Pennine dales. In the upper reaches of the
South Tyne and of the Allen rivers there are heady places
– the highest village, the highest town, the highest pub.
The upper Tees seems lonelier but after it tumbles over
High Force, Teesdale softens until the river provides the
perfect setting for Barnard Castle, a town of fine houses.
Visitors however should travel up not down Teesdale,
climbing up onto the moors until they seem to be on top
of the world.

Allen Banks (63)

Near Plankey Mill. A National Trust property.

Smelt Mill Chimney (64)

At Stublick near Langley.

Near Sinderhope (65)

In Allendale.

The West Allen (66)

Just above its meeting with the East Allen at
Cupola Bridge.

Park Burn (67)

On Plenmeller Common.

Plenmeller Common (68)

Which lies between the rivers West Allen and
South Tyne.

Lambley Viaduct (69)

In the South Tyne valley, with Featherstone
Castle in the distance.

Lambley (70)

A Hexham-to-Alston train leaving Lambley station. The line is now closed but frequently during severe winters it was Alston's only link with the rest of the region.

The South Tyne Valley (71)

From Eals Bridge.

Coalcleugh (72)

Once England's highest village, now
abandoned.

Lead Miners' Cottages (73)

In Upper Weardale, near Nenthead, and the
meeting of the three counties:
Northumberland, Durham and Cumbria.

Farm Buildings (74)

Low Allers, Upper Weardale.

Old Quarry (75)

Near Cowshill, Weardale.

Old Quarry (76)

Near Rookhope, Weardale.

Upper Teasdale (77)

Together with neighbouring Upper Weardale
and Allendale this is a part of Northumbria
where winter arrives early and leaves late.

Holwick Scar (78)

In Upper Teesdale, near Middleton.

Barnard Castle (79)

This large market town marks the beginning of Upper Teesdale. In addition to its medieval castle 'Barney' has many fine eighteenth and nineteenth-century houses, an 'Ancient and Modern' parish church and the chateau-style Bowes Museum.

Raby Castle (80)

A medieval castle set in a landscaped deer-
park, it is the centre of the vast Raby estate
whose whitewashed farms speckle this stretch
of the north Tees countryside.

A Note on the Photography

All the pictures in this book were taken with Pentax Spotmatic SLR cameras; the lenses used with the Pentax were of 35 mm, 55 mm, and 105 mm focal length.

Nearly all the colour transparencies were taken on Kodachrome K64, K25 or, prior to its sad demise in 1975, Kodachrome II. (When this excellent film was superseded by the then inferior Kodachrome 25 and 64 I gave up photography for two years.) A few of the colour slides were taken on Kodak Ektachrome.

In making the final selection of eighty pictures I have tried to strike a balance between the demand in any book of this kind for views of familiar landmarks and my own desire to reveal some of the less obvious attractions of the region. Some readers are going to be disappointed that their favourite building or beauty spot has not been included and I myself regret that there was no room for places such as Kilhope Wheel, Belsay Castle, Ryhope Pumping Station, Gainford Village, Warkworth Castle and the Union Suspension Bridge.

Acknowledgements

The selection is a personal one, although I must acknowledge the critical help of my wife Rosemary; in making a choice between two competing views of the same subject when I dithered she decided. She was also responsible for eliminating a couple of my more 'artistic' efforts.

I should like to acknowledge the advice and practical help I have received from several people including John Laidler and Brenda Owen at Colorworld, Jesmond; all the staff at Bonsers Photographic, Newcastle; Paul McKie and Joe Percy at Ravensworth Studios, Newcastle.

DAVID BELL
The Bookshop
Gosforth
Newcastle upon Tyne
NE3 4AA

Selected Bibliography

ALLSOPP, B., AND CLARK, U., *Historic Architecture of Northumberland and Newcastle Upon Tyne*, Oriel Press 1967, 1969 and 1977

ATKINSON, F., *Life and Tradition in Northumberland and Durham*, J.M. Dent 1977, Dalesman, 1986

BECKENSALL, S., *Northumberland's Pre-historic Rock Carvings*, Pendulum, 1983

BREEZE, DAVID J., and DOBSON, BRIAN, *Hadrian's Wall*, Penguin, 1976

CHARLTON, B., *Story of Redesdale*, Northumberland National Park, 1986

CLIFTON-TAYLOR, A., *Another Six English Towns*, BBC, 1984

— *Six More English Towns*, BBC, 1984

COOPER, HELEN A., *Winslow Homer Watercolours*, Yale University Press, 1986

CROSTHWAITE, R., *Ancient Cleveland from the Air*, Tees Towing Co., 1987

DAVIES, HUNTER, *A Walk along the Wall*, Weidenfeld & Nicolson, 1974

EMBLETON, RONALD, and GRAHAM, FRANK, *Hadrian's Wall in the Days of the Romans*, Frank Graham, 1984

FRASER, GEORGE MACDONALD, *Steel Bonnets: Story of the Anglo-Scottish Border Reivers*, Pan, 1974

GODFREY, LESLIE R.L. (ed), *Complete Northumbria*, Ward Lock, 1979

GORDON, L., *Berwick-upon-Tweed and the East March*, Phillimore, 1985

GRIERSON, E., *Companion Guide to Northumbria*, Collins, 1976

HEPPLE, L.W., *History of Northumberland and Newcastle*, Phillimore, 1976

HOPKINS, T., *Northumberland National Park*, Michael Joseph/Webb & Bower, 1987

MAGNUSSON, MAGNUS, *Lindisfarne*, Oriel Press, 1974

MIDDLEBROOK, S., *Newcastle upon Tyne, Its Growth and Achievement*, Newcastle Journal, 1950

PEVSNER, N., *County Durham* (Buildings of England series), Penguin, 1953

— *Northumberland* (Buildings of England series), Penguin, 1957

— *North Yorkshire* (Buildings of England series), Penguin, 1966

RIDLEY, NANCY, *Northumbrian Heritage*, Robert Hale, 1982

SNELLING, REBECCA, and WENHAM, VALERIE, *Ordnance Survey Leisure Guide to Northumbria*, AA Books, 1987

SOPWITH, T., *Mining District of Alston Moor, Weardale and Teesdale*, Davis Books, 1984

THOROLD, H., *Shell Guide to Durham*, Faber & Faber, 1980

TOMLINSON, W.W., *Comprehensive Guide to Northumberland*, W.H. Robinson, 1888 and Davis Books 1985

WALTON, ROBIN, *History of Coxhoe*, Robin Walton, 1986

WHITE, J.T., *Scottish Borders and Northumberland*, Eyre Methuen, 1973

WHITTAKER, N., and CLARK, U., *Historic Architecture of County Durham*, Oriel Press, 1971

WILSON, J. (ed), *Durham Book*, Durham County Council, 1984